INTRODUCTION

INTRODUCTION

This book is based on advice and guidance that has been shared over time with students. It has been written in response to positive feedback and requests to publish and share more widely. Those who have chosen to follow the advice have found personal success in establishing sound underpinning strategies for learning.

The Students' Guide to Success at Almost Everything seeks to highlight some simple techniques that demystify approaches to learning.

The authors each have over 30 years' experience working with a range of learners in a variety of education and training settings. A brief summary is provided below.

Hugh Smith

Hugh has experience of supporting and encouraging learners from age five to adult years. His experience not only covers Early Years, Primary, Secondary, College and University phases, but also industry trainees in a range of work-based settings and disciplines. He is passionate about learning and encouraging others to learn effectively. Formerly Head of Career-Long Professional Learning within a School of Education in a University and a former head teacher, he continues with consultancy, public speaking, research and writing activities. He is a practising educational technologist and has diverse interests including technology enhanced learning approaches to supporting learning and teaching.

Hugh's main hobbies outside education are photography and making and repairing string instruments.

Helen M Smith

Helen has experience of supporting and encouraging learners from age five to adult years, spanning Early Years, Primary, Secondary and University phases. She is passionate about enhancing and maximising learning opportunities and is a successful learning and teaching practitioner. She is currently a School Enhancement Developer within the university sector.

Helen's main interests lie in education; computing and music and in addition to her learning and teaching activities, is a qualified genealogist, dividing her leisure time between genealogy and crafts.

SMITHSONS
PUBLISHING

STUDENTS' GUIDE TO SUCCESS AT ALMOST EVERYTHING

Hugh Smith and Helen M Smith

Orders:

Please email Smithsons Publishing

admin@smithsonspublishing.com

ISBN: 978-0-9935437-0-8

First published 2016

Printed in Great Britain for Hugh and Helen M Smith by Bell & Bain Ltd, 303 Burnfield Road, Thornliebank, Glasgow G46 7UQ

CONTENTS

ACKNOWLEDGEMENTS

ACKNOWLEDGEMENTS

Illustrations

Pixabay - Creative Commons License Public Domain

Garylarts

H Smith

Publication Advice and Mentoring

Richard McMunn - www.RichardMentorMe.com

HOW TO USE
THIS BOOK

How to Use This Book

This book provides a set of tools and ideas that students have found useful in a variety of learning situations. You may wish to read from beginning to end, dip in and out, or jump to sections that seem most relevant to your situation.

It is not a shortcut or quick fix to completing tasks or solving problems; but rather an exploration into what might become your personal preference for managing the learning process effectively. Ultimately this should boost your confidence and lead to successful achievements time and time again.

Content is divided into four sections; each with a number of topics. "So you think you know about the Internet" is probably worth working through first, as many of the topics are dependent on using skills covered in this section. Each topic is clearly labelled so if you already know (for example) how to download web pages to read offline or search for specific file types on academic sites you can select another topic.

The "How to think like your teacher" section builds on some of the information literacy web skills covered in the first section, by demonstrating through key examples of how your teacher might think when compiling topic content; and creating assignments and examination questions. Essentially, the step by step illustrated guide should develop your knowledge and skills as well as boost your confidence.

The section entitled "The Motivational Bit" explores how to develop communication confidence and avoid the simple errors and misunderstandings made by so many in relation to spoken and written grammar. This is an area that is always problematic for both the inexperienced and experienced learner, so revisiting some simple rules will ensure you develop your knowledge and skills appropriately. Creating the perfect CV is explored; which can be updated and tweaked over time as your skills, knowledge and experience grow. In addition, this section explores why the rules for engagement within social media contexts should never cross over into more formal learning settings.

The "Health and Wellbeing" section explores how to optimise personal mental and physical health which may impact on successful learning. Some common held beliefs are discussed and some simple, effective advice suggested.

Regardless of whether you are a university student, a college student, a senior school student or an adult returner, some or all of the following will apply:

- you will be interacting with key thinkers and practitioners in your chosen subject/s, who will share their professional expertise and also that of others within their national and international networks. You may have limited access to these key thinkers and practitioners, so it is important that you develop skills that would maximise opportunities. This book explores how you might begin to manage and enhance those learning opportunities and develop useful skills and techniques that will ensure personal achievement with a probable future route to employment.

- you will find that a range of help and support is available to you within your institution, which can be accessed when you feel such assistance might be beneficial. Exploring and acting upon the suggestions and advice within this book may provide opportunities for you to ease the transition from school/college/university learning and to make informed choices regarding your own engagement with learning activities and tasks. This will ensure the very best preparation for selection for the workplace or further learning.

- you will currently be exploring subject content and skills that will prepare you for external assessment and national awards. Success for you may be the selection process for the workplace or further learning. This book will provide simple approaches to supporting your own learning requirements over time.

The advice and suggestions within the book sections should encourage you to think about the best way to manage your learning. You may have much to draw on in relation to your personal learning to date, so it is vital that you engage with sections in a way that will be most meaningful to you.

Irrespective of your current learning experience and situation, accessing and registering with the companion website **www.studentspaceuk.com** will provide additional material and resources. A unique aspect to the companion website is an opportunity to share new ideas and tools encountered as part of your learning. Once approved, they may be added to the useful links and resources section of the companion website and may appear in future versions of the book.

SECTION 1

SO YOU THINK YOU KNOW ABOUT THE INTERNET?

SECTION 1 – So you think you know about the Internet?

Most students have heard about Google Scholar, but not many have heard about specialised search engines, the deep invisible web, advanced search techniques, how to set alerts to email you every time keywords are published on the web; and how to access useful web sites that are no longer 'live' - the frustration of the 'Page not found ' message.

This section will cover the following:

• Capturing and downloading web page contents as one file

• Effective web searching (advanced searching by phrase; domain; usage rights)

- Google alerts and Gmail
- Search Engines, Directories, Metacrawlers and Metasearch Engines
- Deconstructing URLs
- Reverse link searching
- Accessing old and outdated weblinks
- Subject Gateways and Databases
- Deep invisible web
- Where to get free stuff
- Free web tools
- Creating a delicious account
- Using Irfanview (and Pixabay)
- How to create a Gmail account

To reduce scope for error when retyping web addresses, it is recommended that you select the weblinks from within the companion website.

Students are often required to attend 'Study Skills', 'Key Skills' or 'Information Literacy' sessions as part of their course. These sessions are often delivered by staff who think they know what is best for the student (without actually asking the student how much they know already or what they need to know for their specific course). From experience, students actually know very little about the 'Internet'. The Internet is in fact the wrong term (but it has commonly become the accepted term when talking about online information and browsing habits). The Internet is essentially the hardware (computers, servers and routers) that connects a "global network" of computers. Accessing online information is enabled through browsing the world wide web (www).

Ask a group of students which search engine they use and over 90% will reply 'Google'. This is interesting, considering there are hundreds of search engines; the categories of which will become clear as we go through this section.

Capturing and downloading web page contents as one file

Here is a neat tool than can capture a set of web pages. This example relates to information about search engines from
http://www.thesearchenginelist.com/

Step 1   Go to the following web address (also known as URL – Uniform Resource Locator) **http://www.pdfmyurl.com**

Step 2   Either type or copy and paste the website address below: **http://www.thesearchenginelist.com/**

Step 3

PDFmyURL
.COM

Pricing   HTML to PDF API   Save as PDF link |

Save web pages as PDF!

Let your visitors turn web pages into PDF with a single click!
Or use our powerful web to PDF API that comes with many options and clear examples.

You'll be making professional PDFs in a few minutes!

LEARN MORE   SIGN UP!

http://www.thesearchenginelist.com/   Options   Save as PDF

Select **Save as PDF**

This provides a copy of a complete webpage rather than a screen shot that only captures the screen area.

Effective web searching (advanced searching by phrase; domain; usage rights)

Everyone knows about Google, so before considering other search engines, directories, metacrawlers and metasearch engines, let us look at what Google can offer in terms of advanced searching.

Step 1   Go to the following web address:
         http://www.google.com/advanced_search

Advanced Search		
Find pages with...		To do this in the search box
all these words:		Type the important words: tricolor rat terrier
this exact word or phrase:		Put exact words in quotes: "rat terrier"
any of these words:		Type OR between all the words you want: miniature OR standard
none of these words:		Put a minus sign just before words you don't want: -rodent, -"Jack Russell"
numbers ranging from:	to	Put 2 periods between the numbers and add a unit of measure: 10..35 lb, $300..$500, 2010..2011

At the right side of the screen, Google provides examples of what you might wish to enter in the search boxes (or 'fields' – to use the correct term).

If searching for information about 'learning theories' you could add this to the field 'all these words' but it would return with over 6 million results (as it matches on 'learning' and on 'theories').

Using **the exact word or phrase** (with quotations) is better as it returns around 592,000 results; however, rather than trawling through every single one of those results and taking pot luck with sites that may contain useful information, it would be advisable to narrow down those results from academic domains such as **.ac.uk** or **.edu**. (By adding another country's domain, you can access useful results such as **.edu.au** for Australia and **.edu.in** for India).

Domain	Country
.au	Australia
.eu	European Union
.af	Afghanistan
.ca	Canada
.za	South Africa
.mt	Malta
.nz	New Zealand
.us	United States
.ie	Ireland

The search for "learning theories" from **.ac.uk** domains narrows the search to around 13,500 results.

Step 2

Advanced Search

Find pages with...

all these words:

this exact word or phrase: learning theories

any of these words:

none of these words:

numbers ranging from: to

Then narrow your results by...

language: any language

region: any region

last update: anytime

site or domain: .ac.uk

terms appearing: anywhere in the page

SafeSearch: Show most relevant results

file type: any format

By narrowing the search further, you can include only searches where "learning theories" appears in the title of the page.

Step 3

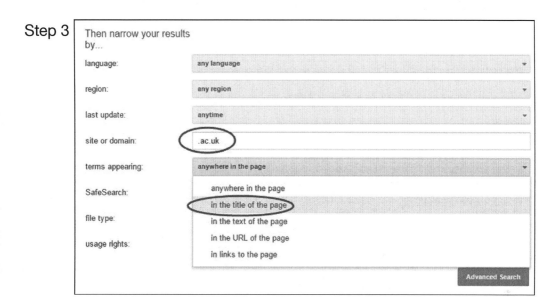

This reduces the number of results to around 151 (at the time of searching), which further reduces the information to scrutinise. Additional text-based search strategies are available on the companion website at **www.studentspaceuk.com**

Further searches may be performed for specific file types. This may be useful when searching for presentations (.ppt), government reports (.pdf), or spreadsheet datasets (.xls) from government sites (.gov.uk).

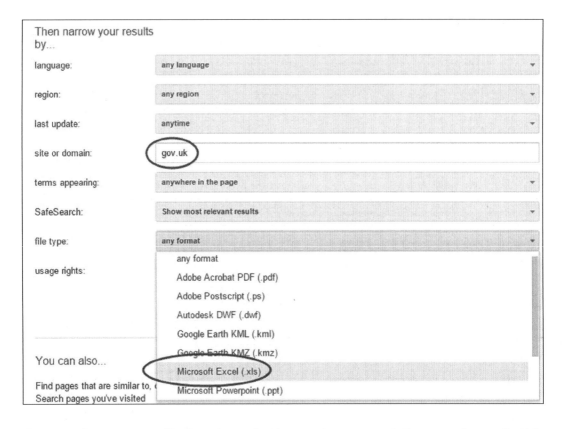

As a student you are likely to be asked to make presentations and usually this would involve the insertion of images. With reference to copyright compliance, you would want your images to be copyright free; probably produced under CC license (Creative Commons). Details of the three levels of license are available at: **https://creativecommons.org/licenses/**

In addition to examples of Google Advanced search techniques below, you can also perform a search on the Creative Commons website for images, videos, text and music at: **http://creativecommons.org/**

Other copyright free sites are discussed later in the free stuff section.

Assume that we want to use a cartoon image of a student. Using a new Google advanced search page, enter **student cartoon** in the 'all these words' field.

Find pages with...

all these words:	student cartoon
this exact word or phrase:	
any of these words:	
none of these words:	
numbers ranging from:	to

Scroll down to: *Then narrow your results by...* section, and *usage rights*

Then narrow your results by...

language:	any language
region:	any region
last update:	anytime
site or domain:	
terms appearing:	anywhere in the page
SafeSearch:	Show most relevant results
file type:	any format
usage rights:	not filtered by license

Select: *free to use or share*

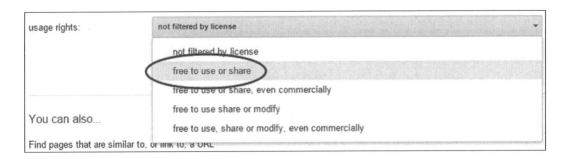

Different countries have different copyright laws, so it is best to select the most appropriate country for your requirements. The following example relates to Canada.

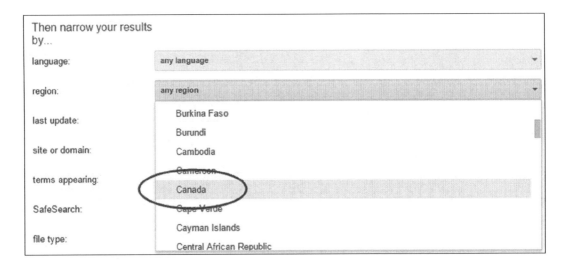

Similar queries may be made for more up to date information by using the *last update* feature …

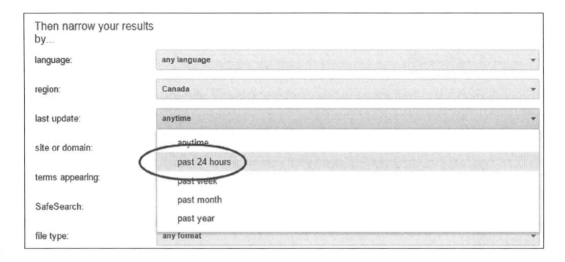

and selecting (for example) – **past 24 hours**. Similar searches may be made for different languages:

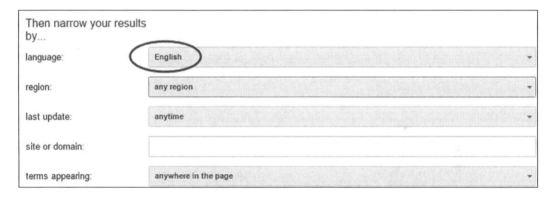

Further examples of using advanced search techniques for supporting assessment are provided in the "How to think like your Teacher " section.

Before leaving Google, there are two further features worth exploring: Google Alerts and Gmail.

Google Alerts and Gmail

Are you aware that alerts can be set up that will email you every time there is an occurrence of key words on a website relating to your topics, interests or hobbies?

Step 1   You will require a personal email account. If you do not have one, follow the instructions for creating a Gmail account at the end of this section.

Go to the following web address: **http://www.google.co.uk/alerts**

Step 2   In the **Search** query box, add your search criteria.

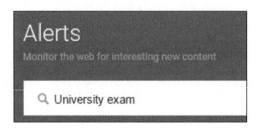

University exam will match on any 'university name' and 'exam' or 'examination'; for example 'Oxford **University Exam**ination'

Step 3   Before selecting CREATE ALERT, go to **Show options**

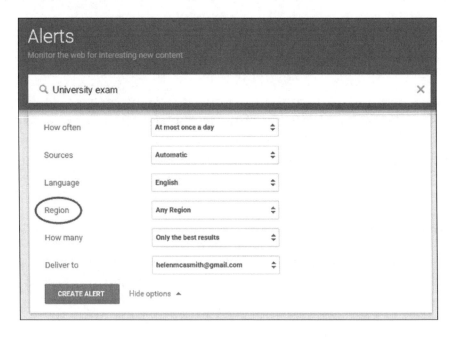

In the **Region** box you can limit the search to United Kingdom (but given that the Language is set to 'English', you might want to leave the Region box as 'Any Region' to capture results from USA, Australia and other English speaking nations). If your first language is not English, then you can select another language.

Add your email address to the **Deliver to** box. It might be worth setting up another email account for this purpose, as the alerts you set up might overfill your existing email in-box. Remember to create a meaningful email address and avoid choosing one that would not impress any future employer. Do you think an employer would employ you with an email like *sexy2shoes@gmail.com* or *pinkfluffyslippers@gmail.com*?

Further information on specialised Google alerts is covered in the 'How to think like your teacher' section.

Search Engines, Directories, Metacrawlers and Metasearch Engines

Although over 90% of students are likely to be using Google, there are many search mechanisms that can produce refined results. Used in conjunction with some of the refined search techniques mentioned previously, these search mechanisms may provide an efficient, speedy way to access a wealth of quality information.

News Search Engines

Current news can be found using your favourite search engine. Where a specific News Search Engine is used, you will find the most up to date information. Search engines are crawling the web constantly to provide the most up to date information. In addition to the specialist search **http://news.google.co.uk** compare the results when searching for a piece of current news at **http://newsisfree.com** and **http://dailyearth.com**

A listing of News Search Engines is provided in the useful links section of the companion website.

Shopping Search Engines

You probably won't have much time or money to use Shopping Search Engines, but if you include comparison search engines in this category, you may find the best possible deals and prices; for example, UK shopping sites such as:

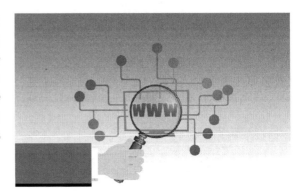

http://ukshop.com

http://pricegrabber.com

http://www.comparestoreprices.co.uk/

A listing of Shopping Search Engines is provided in the useful links section of the companion website.

Multimedia Search Engines (graphics, moving image and audio)

Video or still image formats can be searched using a specialised multimedia search engine. Most know about Google images, but there are other more specialised search engines such as SoundHound and Shazam (for audio). TinEye permits the upload of a picture to perform image recognition and matching, and for video, Youtube still ranks at the top of the video search engines. Blinkx for television and film, still ranks quite highly despite being around for a while; however Blinkx provides access to unique content that you would not find anywhere else.

A full listing of Multimedia Search Engines is provided in the useful links section of the companion website.

Children's Search Engines

There are so many to choose from, but if you have a theme in mind such as children's literature or children's songs, you can locate some really excellent websites such as the Community Learning Network's song lyric search at **http://www.cln.org/themes/songs.html**

A full listing of Children's Search Engines is provided in the useful links section of the companion website.

Country Specific Search Engines

If you require to access a search engine within a specific country, you should access the International Directory of search engines at **http://www.searchenginecolossus.com/**

Japan's list is interesting because it highlights in-country and international websites.

検索デスク(searchdesk)　スタートページ　　　　　　メニュー

ホーム　横断検索　検索　ニュース　SNS　ネット　生活　地域

消

ウェブ検索	ニュース	S N S	ショッピング	地　図
Google 検索	Yahoo! 人気 検索	facebook	Amazon ＊検索	Google 検索
bing 検索	Google 検索	Twitter 検索	楽天市場 ＊検索	Yahoo! 検索
Yahoo! 人気 検索	livedoor goo 人気	Google+ 検索	Yahoo! ＊検索	goo ルート 検索
goo livedoor	Biglobe 人気 @nifty	pixiv mixi	ヤフオク! ＊検索	Mapion ルート 検索
Biglobe @nifty	Infoseek excite msn	LINE GREE	楽オク ＊ebay	いつもNAVI 検索
Infoseek excite	ceek.jp 検索	tumblr. LinkedIn	価格.com 検索	MapFan 検索
msn So-net	米Google 英語	Instagram	ECナビ	bing地図
米Google 英語	米Yahoo! 英語	Pinterest	ヨドバシ ビックカメラ	
米Yahoo! 英語	米reddit 米BuzzFeed		zozotown nissen	
知　識	新　聞	ブ ロ グ	マ ネ ー	乗　換
Y!知恵袋 人気 検索	日経 人気 読売	Yahoo! 人気 goo	日経マーケット IR	Yahoo! 運行
教えて!goo 検索	朝日 産経 人気	楽天 人気 はてなD	Y!ファイナンス 評価	goo 運行
OKWave 人気 検索	毎日 時事 予定	So-net Ameba 人気	米Y!Finance 英語	Jorudan live!
textream 価格.com	47News コラム 社説	livedoor ブログ村	Bloomberg 米国	Navitime 駅探
人力検索 発言小町	東京 CNN ⇒地域	BlogRanking 人気	ロイター 米国	えきから 駅名
Naverまとめ 検索	東京 CNN ⇒地域	JUGEM ココログ	WSJ 米国	ANA JAL LCC
はてなB! 検索	ELOGOS J-cast 人気	excite yaplog	株価 商品	JR東 JR西 JR東海
together AllAbout	BBC CNN NYTimes		日経ビジネス Diamond	都営 メトロ ⇒私鉄
nanapi 米About	FOX WPost USAtoday		東洋経済 Biz-j	
			現代ビジネス Biz誌	

A full listing of Country Specific Search Engines is provided in the useful links section of the companion website.

Metasearch Engines

Dogpile.com (yes – it is actually called that!) is a great example of a metasearch engine that searches across a range of search engines and lists the results. Due to the way indexing works on the Internet, you may occasionally capture information that isn't on Google.

A full listing of Metasearch Engines is provided in the useful links section of the companion website.

Deconstructing URLs

Understanding the structure of a URL (Uniform Resource Locator) – in other words, the web address, may prove to be a very useful skill.

You will be aware that **.ac.uk** denotes an academic domain in the UK for example **http://www.jisc.ac.uk** Similarly, **.sch.uk** denotes a school in the UK. If we delve further into JISC's specific URL for example **https://www. jisc.ac.uk/hairdressing-training** this finds the hairdressing training page on JISC's website.

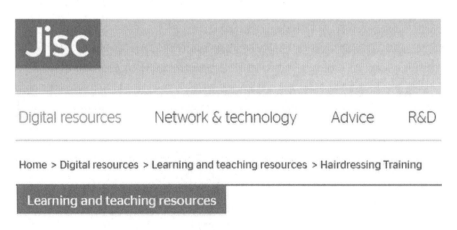

Occasionally, there are personal postings on websites of quality academic domains, which may cause some angst. The tilde character ~ following the domain name denotes a personal page. This personal page is often non-authenticated information sharing personal thoughts and opinions of the author. Even if sites have **.edu** or **.ac.uk** domains, the URL should be scrutinised for the tilde character ~ . If the tilde character ~ is within the URL, think carefully before accepting the information.

There are further examples of hoax websites in the useful links section of the companion website.

Reverse link searching

When validating the credibility of website information it is useful to identify who is linking to that website. This is called reverse link searching and can be useful in determining if the website is credible. The example below illustrates that the website **whitehouse.net** has 8 results that refer to **whitehouse.net** so it is unlikely to be the genuine USA Whitehouse site. To carry out a reverse link search, type **link:** followed by the web address you wish to check.

Accessing old and outdated weblinks

It is extremely annoying when you wish to revisit a webpage at a later date, only to receive the dreaded 404 error message:

Not Found

HTTP Error 404. The requested resource is not found.

All is not lost however, as there is a site called **archive.org** which does exactly as advertised. It archives web pages and it is a **.org** (not for profit organisation). This is USA focused, but the archive at **http://www.webarchive.org.uk/ ukwa/** is UK focused. More examples of how archive.org can help students is discussed in the free stuff section. Archived sites are very useful for viewing previous versions of a website.

Subject Gateways and Databases

Subject Gateways and Databases provide a dedicated area for academic searching. Most school/college/university libraries will have someone dedicated to promoting this resource. Have a look at the following:

http://www.ssrn.com/en/ - The Social Science Network which disseminates social science research and provides links to a number of specialised research networks in each of the social sciences.

http://www.dmoz.org/Regional/Europe/United_Kingdom/ - DMOZ is the largest and most comprehensive human-edited open directory on the Web. It is constructed and maintained by a global community of volunteer editors. It was historically known as the Open Directory Project (ODP).

http://scholar.google.co.uk/ - Google Scholar is a dedicated search engine that searches for academic papers and writings.

http://www.questia.com – Questia provides credible sources that can be cited and referenced. Questia has access to more than 83,000 academic books and more than 10 million articles from more than a thousand of the world's leading publishers.

http://www.sciencedirect.com/ - Science Direct is a leading full-text scientific database offering journal articles and book chapters from over 3,500 journals and more than 34,000 books that are categorised by the different sciences.

http://www.doaj.org – DOAJ is the Directory of Open Access Journals. It is an online directory that indexes and provides access to high quality, open access, peer-reviewed journals.

http://www.proquest.com/libraries/academic/databases/ - Proquest is an academic database that provides a single source for scholarly journals, newspapers, reports, working papers, and datasets along with millions of pages of digitized historical primary sources and more than 450,000 ebooks.

Your library may have some or all of these.

Deep invisible web

Did you know that the content hidden in the **deep web** is rarely found by conventional searches?

Read all about it at: **http://www.webpages.uidaho.edu/~mbolin/ iffat-sami.htm**

(Note that this web address contains the ~ character)

The 'invisible' web is the term given to areas of the world wide web that cannot normally be accessed by search engines as they are not indexed. Some of the databases in libraries are part of this 'invisible' web. Basically, once you land on an information portal, you need to search that database directly for 'deeper' information that is hidden in that database.

Try a search for 'Exam paper' at **www.worldwidescience.org**

This search is particularly useful as it filters the results by country, language and topic. There is also a visual representation of the results.

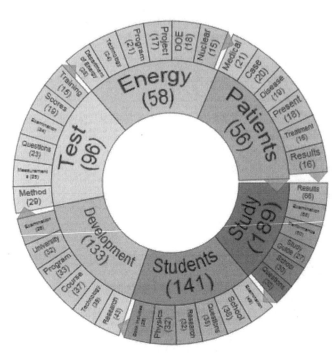

Where to get FREE stuff

Once you have mastered the advanced search techniques, you should be able to search on academic domains for book titles in a **.pdf** format. You may be able to access free text books and free resources. A useful resource which may help with your learning is access to text book companion websites. More detailed information about accessing these free resources is described below.

Step 1   Visit **www.archive.org** and search for free text books. There are 1000s of books, so be selective by searching for **'Illustrated'** which will provide books with diagrams: e.g. **Illustrated Science**

Step 2   Select the book icon to access the text resources.

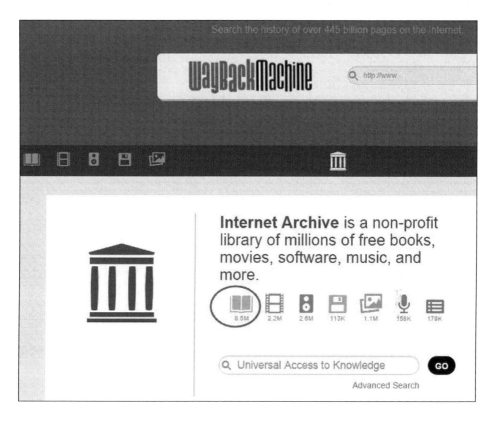

Step 3   Enter the search term "illustrated science" in eBooks and Texts

Step 4   Here is a list of books previously found on archive.org: All URLs are listed in the companion website.

https://archive.org/details/ ChemistryAnIllustratedGuideToScience_514

Chemistry: An illustrated guide to Science with numerous links to related internet sites. A great free resource.

https://archive.org/details/ MammalsbritannicaIllustratedScienceLibrary

A comprehensive book on everything you would wish to know about Mammals from the Britannica Illustrated Science Series.

https://archive.org/details/cu31924074096060

An Illustrated Dictionary of Medicine Biology and Allied Sciences from the Cornell University Library Collection.

https://archive.org/details/ost-biology-the_elements_of_ animal_biology

The textbook Elements of Animal Biology. This text was originally published in 1914 and the content still relevant today.

https://archive.org/details/illustratedhints00schm

An early example of an illustrated text with pen and ink drawings introduced to provide clarity for the reader rather than through narrative alone. Originally published in 1901, it gives a rare insight into the advice being given at the time on exercise and looking after the body.

Some of the most freely available books relate to Health and Science. Most of the books are in the public domain, so copyright restrictions may be more relaxed if you wish to use the diagrams in your academic work.

Have fun browsing the site **archive.org** which has links to other free media.

Other free books available at:

http://books.google.co.uk/

Type *Free Books* into this Google search engine to see what might be of interest.

http://bookboon.com/

Bookboon.com is the world's first online book publisher to provide free textbooks for students. Have fun browsing.

http://www.it-ebooks.info/

ebooks relating to information technology – whether learning programming or using applications. Use the *IT-eBooks Search* link at the bottom of the homepage to search for topics of personal interest.

http://free-ebooks.tradepub.com/category/life-sciences/1208/

Free ebooks on the topics of Biotech; Clinical Laboratory; Drug Discovery; Life Sciences Manufacturing and Pharmaceuticals. There is a general link at the left of the webpage to search *View All Topics* > for non-science subject areas that might be of interest.

http://www.gutenberg.org/

The Gutenburg Project offers over 50,000 free high quality ebooks: free epub books, free kindle books, that all can be downloaded and read online.

http://www.bartleby.com/index.html

An Internet Publisher of literature, reference and verse providing students and researchers with unlimited access to books and information on the web free of charge.

http://www.ipl.org/div/subject/

ipl2 was an American public service organisation and a learning/teaching environment. Although the service is no longer updated and now closed, access to free e-resources and links to other useful websites is still available.

http://www.digital.library.upenn.edu/books/

The Online Books Page. This is a website that facilitates access to over two million online books that are freely readable over the Internet. There are also links to directories and archives of online texts.

http://www.ibiblio.org/

ibiblio is one of the largest "collections of collections" on the Internet and is an online public library with freely available software and information, for topics such as music, literature, art, history, science, politics, and cultural studies. With between 12 million to 16 million worldwide transactions per day, it is a resource used frequently by audiences of all interests and backgrounds.

http://www.loc.gov/rr/rarebook/

Some 800,000 books, broadsides, pamphlets, theatre playbills, title pages, prints, posters, photographs, and medieval and Renaissance manuscripts from the American Library of Congress *Rare Book and Special Collections Division.* The collection offer scholarly documentation about the western and American traditions of life and learning. There are other free resources available from Public Domain collections.

http://www.nypl.org/collections

Extensive Collections based at the New York Public Library USA.

https://librivox.org/

Free public domain audiobooks.

Find out where to get free stuff, simply by subscribing to the newsletter at:

http://www.freestuff.com

A website that provides links to a range of free stuff that is updated on a daily basis.

There are many opportunities to be gleaned from repurposing some free Public Domain resources such as making Posters (from old out of print books; old sheet music covers; record sleeves)… the list is endless.

Download free public domain films from:

https://archive.org/details/movies

The Moving Image Archive library contains digital movies uploaded by Archive users which range from classic full-length films, to daily alternative news broadcasts, to cartoons and concerts. Many of these videos are available for free download.

https://scotlandonscreen.org.uk/

Scotland on Screen contains hundreds of films to watch, discuss and use as inspiration for projects.

http://www.archif.com/

The National Screen and Sound Archive of Wales

Free web tools

This section will be supplemented by user-guides and videos from the companion website. There are many free software tools that can make your life so much easier as a student. In this section we are going to examine three tools:

- Delicious – for sharing bookmarks

- IrfanView- for manipulating images

- Pixabay- for sourcing copyright free images

(See also **More Free Stuff** in the 'How to think like your Teacher' section and **Even more free** stuff in the 'Health and Wellbeing' section).

Creating a Delicious account

There are similar tools around, but this is one of the simplest to create and use.

Step 1   Enter **http://delicious.com** in the search bar, then select **Sign Up**

(If you don't have an email account, see 'Creating a Gmail Account' at the end of this section); otherwise, sign up with your email, FaceBook, Twitter or Google account.

Step 2   Once you have registered, you should see a screen similar to this:

Welcome to Delicious!
Delicious and Delicious Mail are the best ways to find and securely share the best content online.

From the menu bar at the left of the screen, select **+Add Link**

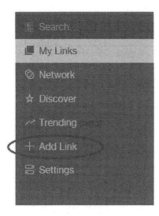

Step 3   Add one of your useful web links then tag and save. For example, if you wish to bookmark the companion website, enter **www.studentspaceuk.com** then select **Add link.**

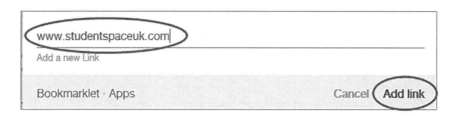

Step 4   You will be prompted to add a title and tags. Enter Students Guide to Success at Almost Everything website and add the tags freestuff, companion_book. (Separate each of the tags with commas) then **Save link**

Step 5   This may appear to be a bit laborious at first, but the advantages will be evident later on when you begin networking with others sharing related information through tags; for example, if you select your tag **freestuff** it will link to others also sharing freestuff.

By selecting the **#freestuff on Delicious**, other shared sites will appear. If you wish to add some of those to your Delicious account, simply click on the link to check out the site (as some may no longer be live) and select **add link**. This will automatically save the link to your Delicious account and add the site to the freestuff tag.

Step 6   *Networking*

By selecting the Network option from the menu at the left of the screen, you can share information and join Networks. Browse through the people and their descriptions and only follow those that have a profile worth following! It may be advisable at this stage, to search by tags and build up a set of links before networking.

This selection of tags provides an overview of interests (mainly educational) but at first glance, the tag for Genealogy stands out. The more web links, the larger the letters in the tag cloud.

Step 7   Search for the account of **StudentSpaceUK** and join the network. You'll have access to all the websites in this book and many more.

Using Irfanview (and Pixabay)

Irfanview is a freeware graphics application which is useful for editing and cropping images; manipulating photographs; and viewing graphics that support multiple file formats.

Step 1   Download and install Irfanview on your computer.

(It is free from **http://www.irfanview.com/**

Step 2   Accept the Cnet download option. (Make sure you only download the Irfanview Application and ignore all the other advertising that may pop up).

Step 3   After downloading and installing, launch Irfanview, then select **Open** from the **File** Menu:

Step 4   Browse and load the graphic image of your choice. This image is a copyright free image downloaded from **www.pixabay.com**

Pixabay is a great resource for accessing images. Simply sign up at **http://www.pixabay.com** (it's free) and search for a theme / topic / image, download to your computer. Ensure that you have selected **CC Public Domain**.

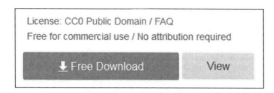

License: CC0 Public Domain / FAQ
Free for commercial use / No attribution required

⬇ Free Download   View

Step 5   Click, hold and drag an area you wish to crop on your image.

Step 6   From the **Edit** menu, select **Crop Selection**

Step 7   **Save** file.

Step 8   **To reduce the image** file size, select **Resize/Resample** from the **Image** menu.

Step 9   From this window, you can reset the Width and Height and the number of pixels (e.g. 640 x 480). Select **Half** or **Double** should you wish.

Save file again. By right clicking on the file icon and selecting **Properties**. You should see a considerable reduction in the file size.

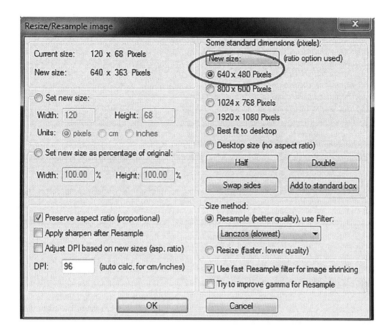

All examples discussed are available either as downloadable user guides or demonstration videos from the companion website.

How to create a Gmail account

Enter **http://mail.google.com**

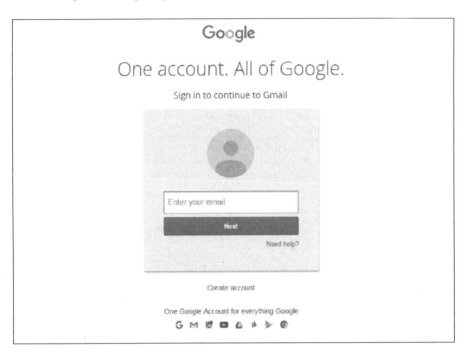

Select **Create account**

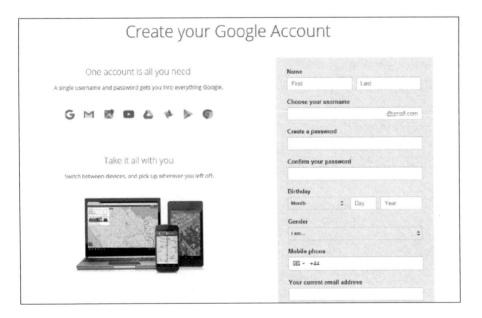

Enter the information in the required boxes (and make a note of your newly created email address and password).

_____@gmail.com

Once you have completed all the required details, you will be shown a screen with YOUR email address.

SECTION 2

HOW TO THINK LIKE YOUR TEACHER

SECTION 2 – How to think like your Teacher

This section will cover:

- Cracking the code to think like your teacher
- Why students fail
- Think like your teacher (examinations)
- Think like your teacher (constructing the examination paper)
- How to access easy to understand sources
- More FREE STUFF
- How to pass exams and assessments at the very first attempt
- Creating a presentation in five minutes
- Teachers' Knowledge

For simplicity, the terms 'student' and 'teacher' are used here to denote any situation where the student is the 'learner' and the 'teacher' is the lecturer/leader of learning.

Cracking the code to think like your teacher

Ask students what they worry about most in terms of their learning and 99% of them will answer "exams and assessment". Despite outlining what ought to be taught on a specific course (and therefore 'learned' by the student), students still haven't cracked the code of being a step ahead in the game and 'thinking like their teacher'. Basically, it is as simple as that! Think of the overworked teacher who reads through a new syllabus and sees a variety of topics (some of which they may not know very much about). This does happen! What do you think they do? They read books; search the world wide web; watch self-help videos; undertake training courses or attend in-service courses.

This section will encourage you to *think like your teacher.* Teachers may know more than you, but probably not as much as you think. Course content often changes every year, so for the teacher, it is a constant battle to keep on top of their subject and identify ways of learning new things.

Students worry about assessment because they fear the unknown. If the assessment is an examination, they worry even more which is surprising, as there are usually lots of past examination papers available in libraries or on-line. If the assessment is an assignment/course-work it may be difficult determining what the teacher is looking for.

Why students fail

- Ambiguous examination questions (what you think the question means, isn't actually what the teacher is looking for or what the teacher intended when setting the question). Teachers have subject knowledge but not all are experienced in setting examination/assessment questions. This is one reason why students fail and why schools/colleges/universities implement moderation procedures.

- Not reading the question properly (or misinterpreting the question)

- Not attending, not undertaking supplementary reading, not engaging, lack of effort.

Think like your teacher (Examinations)

Teachers often have to make up examination papers (and not only that, they usually have to design the re-assessment paper at the same time).

The teacher looks at the syllabus and writes down some key subject knowledge headings. The subject knowledge has to be assessed, but don't think for a minute

that this is going to be a straightforward descriptive type of question such as "What is a..."; "Describe..." "State....". Usually the knowledge type questions have a problem solving element where you need to 'know' something, to be able to answer the question in such a way that 'applies' that knowledge to a specific situation.

Think like your teacher – constructing the examination paper

Q: How might a teacher construct an examination paper?

A: search the world-wide web for examples of examination questions on a particular topic/theme; or read a text book and make up the questions.

Given that teachers may not know how to do advanced searches of academic sites or from hidden databases, you might find yourself at an advantage (see Section 1 of this book on how to do this).

What else might teachers do?

- They would go through the syllabus or module descriptor and write down the key words

- They would search other academic sites for information

- They would look at past papers and edit one or two previous years' questions (likely)

- They would create new questions of their own (unlikely).

- Set students the task of creating questions (good activity as students then find out how hard it actually is!)

So why don't YOU

- go through the course outline and write down all the keywords. If there is something that you simply don't understand, find a source that provides a simpler explanation. (Think of the success of the 'Dummies Guide to...'

books; or information presented from Youtube).

- Search on the video channels for 'easy to understand' movies on all difficult concepts.

The following example came from a former teacher who worked with students in a student attainment capacity. Many former teachers and learning developers/learning support assistants are required to work with students across a range of subjects. Whilst they may not have subject knowledge on every subject, they do have knowledge about learning and the strategies required to be an effective learner. A student had failed a chemistry examination (twice) and was now on the third and final attempt. Feedback was required on the examination which comprised three essay type questions; one of which was about *Chromatography*. Being a non-scientist, the support teacher could see that the student had failed to answer adequately a twenty mark question about chromatography. Although knowing absolutely nothing about chromatography, the support teacher could see that the question required subject knowledge about chromatography but in addition, it required knowledge of how it was applied to a specific situation. The student had written a few sentences on what chromatography *was* and only gained 3 out of 20 for the few facts that had been stated. It didn't take a brain surgeon to work out that a few sentences with a few facts wouldn't gain a huge number of marks (although this did appear to be news to the student!); so with a few strategies to extract exactly WHAT was being asked, the student managed to construct a model answer that explained briefly about chromatography (as that subject knowledge was necessary). With the support of the teacher further reading was identified from a variety of sources. (Section 3 on how to read academic texts will provide a step by step guide on how to extract relevant information).

Try working this example about chromatography (then applying the steps to your area of knowledge).

How to access easy to understand sources:

- Search Youtube or Vimeo for chromatography. The key word **'chromatography'** (at the time of writing) appears in seven videos on Khan Academy, 156 videos on Vimeo and over 26,000 on Youtube. Despite what you may think about some of these sources (including Vimeo and YouTube) there is a wealth of information which, providing it is backed up with relevant academic sources, may provide a useful starting point.

- Check out Wikipedia AND the list of references supporting the information. Obviously, if articles are not referenced, then avoid them. Always go to the source and CHECK that the information is as referenced.

- Using the search strategies discussed in Section 1, the keyword 'chromatography' (using a simply search) will match on over 32 MILLION sources, which is perhaps a few more than we would like at this stage. Using the advanced search techniques, this  can be narrowed down to 241,000 if searching on academic sites in the UK only (.ac.uk domains). Chromatography even has its own journal!

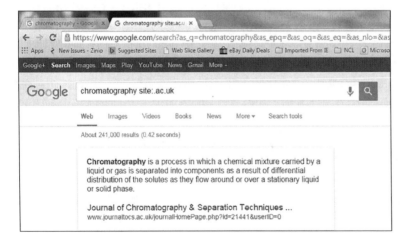

This is all very interesting but how can we access examples of questions (and more to the point – the sample answers?)

Once you have exhausted all the search techniques and searched across academic sites in different countries using the **.edu** and **.edu.au** domains, try adding different keywords to search specifically for examination questions.

Additional weblinks relating to exam questions are available on the companion website **http://www.studentspaceuk.com**

Incidentally, the American academic sites have over 858,000 sources on chromatography and one university has its own 'wiki' called Chemwiki.

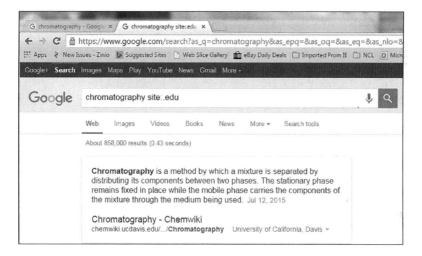

The Australian academic search results in over 31,400 sources and the top level hits provide a link to another journal and a free book chapter. On further investigation, the free Chapter contains worked solutions to questions from an advanced chemistry textbook. Refining the search terms further to include 'questions' and 'solutions' may return some interesting results.

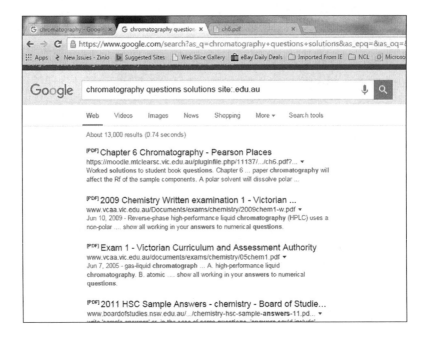

More FREE STUFF

Many ebooks and recently published text books have linked **companion web sites**, or sections containing revision *questions and answers*. Check out all the books in the library relating to your subject as there may be a questions and answers section in the book that would be worth investigating. Teachers are busy people, so they may have taken the same shortcuts in making up your examination paper!

Download (or copy from Library files) all the previous years' examination papers. Identify all the key words in the questions such as 'discuss'; 'explain';

'critically evaluate'; 'outline'; 'state'; and 'describe'; then practise writing the solutions. The topic for exam questions will likely be the same from year to year, but it is important that you READ the question carefully as it may have key words such as 'explain why', 'discuss how', 'critically evaluate'.

If your assessment is an item of coursework, make sure you get a librarian or student support tutor to provide feedback on the structure of your assignment and the format of your referencing. Don't lose valuable marks because of poor referencing. Check you have used the resources on the reading list; especially if your teacher has written some of the books! The course outline will have listed all the reading you are expected to have undertaken, so make sure you read, use (and reference) these resources. A quick guide to referencing is available from the companion website.

Companion website examples:

The following examples can be accessed from the useful links section of the companion website.

http://www.pearsoninternationaleditions.com/Sitemap/Brookshear/

Some books have free companion sites, for example

http://highered.mcgraw-hill.com/sites/0073532223/information_center_view0/sample_chapter.html

and some have free downloadable chapters.

Look for interactive quizzes, free chapters and notes from

http://bcs.whfreeman.com/bps7e/#937162__937199__

Search for your own subject's "companion website" and see the wealth of resources there, including lots of extra questions and solutions which you may use for practising.

See   **http://global.oup.com/booksites/content/9780198507185/student** for mathematical solutions.

By searching for YOUR own subject and companion website, there will be many resources to help in your search for the ideal answers. Similarly, a search for sample chapters may provide some additional resources. Make use of your library's ebooks too, as often a few pages can be printed so those end of chapter questions and answers sections should be useful.

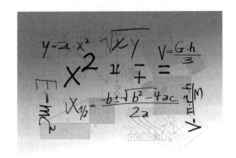

Teachers need to make up the questions and assignments so ensure you know exactly what each keyword means. It is unlikely that you would get a straightforward 'knowledge' type question such as "What is chromatography?" but it is likely that you will need to know what it *is* to help you answer more difficult questions and apply the knowledge to ANY situation which is requested in the exam.

How to pass exams and assessments at the very first attempt

Now that we have some strategies to source information about specific topics that might be assessed, how can we guarantee success at the very first attempt? The solution is relatively simple IF you are willing to 'play the assessment' game. This involves actually starting on the assessment as soon as it is issued. At every session with your teacher, ask pertinent questions to try and ascertain exactly in which format the teacher wants the information. This is useful if it's an essay, presentation or report. If there are support groups or tutorials, ATTEND! It is amazing how many of these support sessions are offered but few students attend. You can often glean additional bits and pieces of information not offered elsewhere. Go prepared with questions and if available, get feedback on your work. Every teacher wants their students to succeed. Before submitting, check your writing and if necessary use the additional support staff for planning, structuring, grammar, syntax and referencing.

Don't second guess what is required. Read the assignment brief carefully and if any aspects are not clear, ASK QUESTIONS! (Typical questions include 'should I write in the first person?'; 'is it an essay or report writing style?')

By adopting some of the search techniques mentioned in the previous section, you will acquire a fair amount of knowledge. Start simply then build up to more complex reading. Above all, answer the assessment question that has been asked.

Using information from the previous section, set up a Google alert on your assessment topic.

Creating a presentation in 5 minutes

This topic isn't really about cutting corners to produce a presentation in five minutes. You want to produce quality stuff as easily as possible and in the shortest time so it is necessary to be a bit more strategic in doing so. Consider a topic. It doesn't matter which topic is selected as the strategies deployed below will work for ANY topic.

Presentations are often long and boring, despite being factual. Too often, the slides are over-crowded and the presenter reads word for word from the screen. If asked to create a presentation, save time and effort by searching for existing presentations on the topic and repurpose the information extracted. At the very least, you can save time and effort if the examples downloaded have already been referenced.

The old mantra: tell them what you are going to say; say it; then say it again holds true for any presentation structure. Following the same search principles in Section 1, conduct an advanced search for presentations only (for example .ppt for Powerpoint) on a given topic. In this example, a presentation is going to be constructed about 'Google Tools'. A few existing presentations are going to be sought to capture a flavour of style and content and then templates and themes will be selected to complement the content.

Worked Example:

Two ways to find examples of existing presentations

1. Search and download examples of presentations on your topic at

    http://www.slideshare.net/

2. Perform an advanced search for all presentations on your topic. Download a few as examples. (You may need to search for specific file types such as **.ppt** and on specific domains such as **.ac.uk** or **.edu**).

Use a free simple tool (Google Slides) to create the presentation if you don't have access to software such as Powerpoint.

https://docs.google.com/presentation/

A user guide on creating a slide show is available from the companion website.

Teachers' Knowledge

Teachers' knowledge is likely to fall under one of the following categories:

*   Subject Knowledge

*   Pedagogic Knowledge

*   School Knowledge

Some have great subject knowledge, are inspired by their subject, and usually make teaching fascinating for their students. Pedagogic knowledge is where the teacher utilises their expertise and manages to break that knowledge down into meaningful episodes for the purpose of helping you (the learner) to understand the concepts and content. School knowledge – well basically that's keeping a step ahead of what's in the syllabus to get by on a daily basis. Unfortunately there are a few teachers around that fall into this category.

You've heard the aphorism by George Bernard Shaw "He who can, does. He who cannot, teaches."

Following an assignment at the end of a topic, one teacher has the students correct their own papers by applying the marking scheme and determining their final grade. Another teacher marks the assignment provides the students with their marks and tells them where they went wrong.

Which is the best method for motivating the students? Which is the best process for helping the students to learn? Which would you prefer?

In a later section we will look at motivation, mindsets and building confidence, but for a moment, let's go back to how you might think like your teacher in making a difficult aspect of learning 'easy' for students. The chromatography example was a bit extreme, but was as good an example as any to start with. Teachers are required to teach difficult concepts and are often challenged by students uttering *"Why are we doing this?" "Why do we need to learn this?" "This is boring"*. One such example is floating point numbers and the need for mathematical precision. (Not an easy concept to teach or explain!) After weeks of constant *"this is boring" "Why do need to know this"* – and trying to avoid the old worn cliché *"it's in the exam syllabus so just learn it"*, students were set the task of creating a learning object (or seeking out an existing learning object) that they could repurpose and use to teach others about the difficult concept. See this example on Youtube.

Learning binary (Fun Binary Conversion):

https://www.youtube.com/watch?v=y0BOA1JX8W4

This further example uses an existing video for demonstration.

Why precision numbers and calculation are important:

https://www.youtube.com/watch?v=EZNpnCd4ZBo

You should be able to see the similarity between *you* as the learner and the teacher. Both teacher and student have to go through the same stages when learning new things. Forget about putting teachers on pedestals as all they are doing is repurposing the subject knowledge into meaningful chunks to help you learn; however, some are better at this than others.

SECTION 3

THE MOTIVATIONAL BIT!

Section 3 – The MOTIVATIONAL bit!

This section will cover:

- how your 'mindset' can affect the way you learn

    - determining your mindset

    - intrinsic and extrinsic motivation

- confidence building strategies

    - don't let your grammar let you down

    - the perfect CV

    - the perfect application letter

    - the perfect interview

- making sense of academic writing

    - academic writing and academic reading

How your 'mindset' can affect the way you learn

Today's students often lack confidence. The myth that students learn best when the learning is 'learner centred', 'technology enhanced', 'discovery', 'problem based', 'on-line', does much to undermine student confidence, as well as demoralise the role of the teacher as a subject expert. When used in isolation, it is little more than educational rhetoric. Whilst there is much to commend these 'new approaches', there is nothing that can replace the role of a teacher who is expert in their field and who can impart their knowledge in such a way that motivates and inspires learners. This is what separates the competence based 'good' or 'satisfactory' teacher from the 'outstanding' teacher. Anyhow, enough about teachers. (If you wish to read more about subject knowledge, view the article on the companion website). This introduction is simply to set the scene in order to encourage a love of your subject(s) and encourage **you**, the student to see the relevance of the subject in your life. You cannot always leave it up to a teacher to make those connections for you. If they are unable to repurpose the subject content, then some of the above statements about 'leaner-centred' may be true after all. You decide – when you feel more confident to do so.

What kind of student are you?

Determining your mindset.

STUDENT A	STUDENT B
I got a grade A because I am clever; because I worked hard; I'll get a grade A the next time, because I am still clever. I am confident and I know everything. I am very smug.	I failed because Mr Bloggs hates me; or the stuff I studied didn't come up in the exam; or it was someone else's fault; or my personal life is chaos; it's not my fault – it's everyone else's fault! The teacher was rubbish. The dog chewed my computer.

OK – the above examples are extreme, but most of us, if we are honest, know or recognise someone who falls into one of those categories. Do you recognise yourself? You need to be realistic and be determined to take control. It is what *you*, the learner actually does that enables learning BUT this requires creating the right conditions under which learning can take place. If this isn't provided by the teacher, then *you* need to assume that responsibility for yourself. You can do this!

Intrinsic and Extrinsic Motivation

Intrinsic motivation comes from internal causes – striving to pass your driving test for example. You will sit this over and over again because you really want to drive. You may not like the process of learning to drive, the theory test, the studying but you are determined to have a car and be able to drive so all other negative thoughts are cast aside.

Extrinsic motivation has external causes; not necessarily performed out of self interest (other than through necessity, such as working in a dull job to be paid at the end of the week). Other examples are social approval (being accepted; dressing like your friends), rewards, or avoiding negative consequences. Boredom, lack of confidence and life's transition points are issues for most of us.

The psychologist Carol Dweck states that people's self theories about intelligence have a profound influence on their motivation to learn. See more about Carol Dweck on the companion website at **www.studentspaceuk.com**

Which do you believe?

- intelligence is fixed?

- intelligence can be developed?

GROWTH MINDSET	FIXED MINDSET
- abilities can be developed	- need to look clever at all times
- lifelong learners	- fear failure
- 'Tell me when I am wrong, because I want to learn' mentality	- must get the best grade at all costs
- **all about effort**	- 'Tell me how bright I am' mentality
	- all abo**ut blame**

What the research says:

• If you praise for *intelligence* and students do not meet the mark, they lose confidence

• If you praise for *effort*, confidence is maintained

  (Dweck, 2007).

See the news article at **http://www.bbc.co.uk/news/magazine-13128701**

- Praise the effort

- Make learning challenging

- Encourage a mindset that learns from mistakes

- Provide tools to help students become confident learners

- Bounce back from setbacks

- Build confidence and self esteem

- The more you use your brain, the stronger it gets

- Stretch yourself to learn something new (neurons form new connections)

- Growth of mind is (to a large extent) in your hands

In summary: It is *your* willingness to learn that determines how much learning takes place. The right environment is necessary, as well as intrinsic motivation (willingness and interest to learn), personal constructions of meaning through the use of learning strategies (which we hope this book provides) and the need for self-direction. So let's get on with it.

Confidence Building Strategies

Don't let your grammar let you down!

There's no point in reading further until you waken up and do something about all those grammatical structures that you probably don't even realise you may be using wrongly. Pedants (nit pickers) get quite upset when people misplace an apostrophe never mind when they drop the occasional clanger, usually at the most inopportune moment (such as during an interview or making a presentation or public speech). Pedants are also unforgiving as they are often dismissive of someone's intelligence. Please note: not knowing what you don't know in terms of grammatical structure and syntax (arrangement of words) are not signs of poor intelligence. The most intelligent people get it wrong sometimes; and often 'wrong' grammar is used for special effect in dramatic productions and in writing. None of this applies to you however! NOTE –the use of 'applies' is correct here as the word 'none' denotes 'not one' (so singular). Confused? – then read on…..

When a child uses the wrong word (called a malapropism), it is usually very funny; but not so when it's you and you are not aware that people are laughing at you or worst still, are dismissive of you as an educated person. This may not be doing much for your confidence right now in the confidence building section of this book, but that will change once you read and absorb the following:

Use of the apostrophe:

"If in doubt, miss it out" – better to have no apostrophe than a misplaced apostrophe.

Normally, apostrophes indicate ownership (or omitted letters as in **don't**); but be careful not to use them simply when the word is plural. As with all things, there are some exceptions where it would just be absurd if you were to use an apostrophe:

Missing letters: DVDs – is better without the apostrophe to denote the missing letters or it would look like D'V'D'S which is just ridiculous. Don't use an apostrophe in DVDs, CDs, TVs, and other similar words.

It is correct however, to use an apostrophe for words like don't; can't; shouldn't;

Possessive case: This can be a nightmare!

The pupils' schoolbags – denotes more than one pupil (apostrophe after the s)

The pupil's school bag – denotes one pupil (apostrophe before the s)

However: *The children's schoolbags is correct* (as 'children' is classed as a singular group of pupils). Similarly: *the family is in turmoil (not the family are….).* If you are concerned, rework the sentence (for example): *the family members are...*

Examples such as: *the government, the family, everybody,* must be followed by verbs in the singular for example:

The government is cutting taxes.

The family is going on holiday,

Everybody is singing in the choir.

You get the idea?

Possessive and missing letters: It's and its:

It's is used when you mean "**it is**" to indicate the omitted i. **Its** is used to indicate something belonging to it (there is no apostrophe for its. In fact there is no apostrophe for those possessive cases such as its, theirs, ours, yours, hers)

When you are in restaurants and cafes, try spotting misplaced apostrophes. These usually appear on signage outside shops or on menus in cafes. Words like *Coffee's Tea's Potato's Tomato's* - ALL WRONG – but once you know and recognise this fact, you'll begin to see misused apostrophes everywhere!

Words that sound similar but have different meanings:

Affect / effect	This is a difficult one as **affect** is the verb and **effect** is normally the noun; however, you can *effect* change. Clearer examples are: *The country was affected by the storm.* *The special effect was outstanding.* *To effect change, we need to recycle.*

Complement / compliment	Complement – meaning the number or whole part of something. Compliment – for saying something nice about someone. *There was a full complement of staff at the meeting.* *She paid him a compliment when she tasted his cooking.*
Discrete / discreet	Discrete is distinct, whereas discreet is subtle, for example: *The discrete values in the bar graph show the annual results.* *They had a discreet affair which no one knew about.*
Formally / formerly	*It was a formal occasion and they were formally introduced.* (Formally indicates a sense of ceremonial occasion). *He was formerly a head teacher at another school.* (Formerly indicates a previous time).
It's and **its** can be confusing:	It's = stands for it is. Its = the possessive case (belonging) *It's a horrible day today as it has been raining for hours.* *The book was in its gift wrapping when it fell in the puddle.*

Knew / new	*Knew – as past tense of knowing something or someone.* *e.g. He knew that the she had fallen as she was cut and bruised.* *New – as in not old.* *e.g. She has a new coat.*
Know / no	*Know – as in knowing someone or something.* *No – a refusal to do something.*
Led /lead	Led by the collar, he was marched away. Lead piping is installed in old houses. (both pronounced the same way) Lead (pronounced the same as seed) is the usage when guiding or leading the way: e.g. *The drummer will lead the way when the band marches down the street.*
Lose / loose	*If you lose your keys, you will be locked out.* *If the elastic is loose, you'll lose your trousers!*
Past / passed	Past as a noun e.g. Historical events are in the past; or as an adjective e.g. *I am past caring about what you do after work.* Passed is the past tense of the verb 'pass'. *I have passed all my exams with distinction.*

Practice / Practise	Practice (noun) e.g. *I attend choir practice on Mondays.* (C for choir which is the noun) *I like practising my singing.* (S for singing which is a verb)
Principal / Principle	Principal is the spelling used when talking about the principal of a school or college. Principle is the spelling when discussing standards or beliefs. e.g *The rules were drawn up based on sound principles.*
Stationary / Stationery	*The car drew to a halt and was stationary.* *Paper clips, envelopes and paper are in the stationery cupboard.* (Think of *e* for envelope to help you remember the spelling)
There/their/they're	Use 'there' for the position of an object (think of it as 'here and there' meaning over **there** if you have trouble remembering this). The word 'their' indicates possession such as their coats were very *warm*. Think of *i* as being personal. There are many more examples on the companion website. They're – denotes 'They are' with the apostrophe indicating the missing 'a'.
To/too/two;	Number 2 is **two**; **Too** is used for emphasis such as too cold; too hot; too thick); and everything else is 'to'. *I am going to the theatre.*
Whose / who's	Whose (possession) e.g *Whose boots are these?* Who's (denotes missing letters) e.g. *Who is going to the party?* (Who's going to the party)

Grammar and Syntax – most common errors

Using "I seen" which is WRONG.

Think: He saw, she saw, they saw, I saw. All CORRECT.

I have seen, they have seen, he has seen, she has seen. All CORRECT.

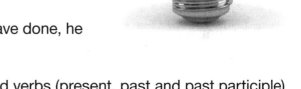

I done – which is WRONG.

Think: I did, she did, they did, he did. All CORRECT.

I have done, she has done, they have done, he has done. All CORRECT.

A table of the most commonly used verbs (present, past and past participle) is available on the companion website.

Other Miscellaneous Things!

Less or fewer? Use fewer when there is a discrete number. For example: *"Fewer students attended the rally this year"*. Use less when there is an unknown quantity. *"There was less rain this week than last week"*.

You can use "consist of" or "comprise" (but it is poor English to use "comprise *of*")

The use of "could have" e.g. *"I could have danced all night"*. Is CORRECT; (NOT "could of").

Tautology – the repetition of the same idea in different words, for example:

"The artist produced a painting that was original and very unique".

"There is no admittance charge for this building. You can enter for free and for nothing at no cost". – OK – this example is a bit extreme, but you get the idea.

Pleonasm – the use of words additional to those from which the meaning is already clear:

"I have seen it with my own eyes".

"We went on a walking tour on foot".

"There is a burning fire in the grate".

The perfect CV

- Is professional

- Doesn't contain a photo! – unless specifically requested

- Is concise (and doesn't ramble on for pages and pages)

- Is truthful

- Has no missing dates/names/signatures/references

- Is free from errors such as typos, grammatical howlers

- Acknowledges the 'person specification' requirements in the 'additional information' section

- Is laid out in neat columns, consistent formatting, type size and font.

Example CV formats can be accessed from the companion website.

The perfect application letter

- **Dear Sir/ Madam**… is concluded by **Yours faithfully** (NOTE small letter at faithfully; not a capital letter)

- **Dear Mr Bloggs** … is concluded by **Yours sincerely** (Again NOTE the small letter and spelling of sincerely)

- Proof read! Typos are unacceptable and careless.

Example letter formats can be accessed from the companion website.

The perfect interview

- Prepare a response to the first question which is (usually) – tell us a bit about yourself and your experience to date; and how this prepares you for this job

- dress appropriately – smart, neat and tidy, no heavy makeup,

- Body language – hands out of pockets; sit up and don't slouch, make eye contact, try not to flap your hands around too much!

- Prepare responses to questions about your skills and personal qualities. Be careful with this type of question as you need to identify the difference between *SKILLS* and *QUALITIES*. As a rough guide, the list below outlines *SKILLS* (something you have learned to do) and *QUALITIES* (traits that you possess as part of your personality)

SKILLS

Effective communication skills (written and oral); Secure computing skills; Creative skills (being able to generate new ideas); Leadership skills; Organisational skills; Time management skills; Presentation Skills.

QUALITIES

Good sense of humour; Patient and tolerant; Flexible; Firm but fair; Reliable; Honest; Good team player; Confident; Responsible; Ambitious.

Making sense of academic writing

Before you can write academically, you need to know HOW to extract information from the books, journals and sites that you read. Your teacher will constantly be telling you to write more critically, more academically, use more referencing, etc. This doesn't mean a whole lot if you don't know HOW to go about it. There are many study skills books and numerous websites but there is no substitute for a worked example that demonstrates the step by step process of a teacher reading an article and talking through the thought processes by providing details on how, when and where to make notes and what to write down. Thinking aloud is a very useful method of demonstrating a specific line of thinking when reading academic texts. There are worked examples on the companion website.

Academic writing and academic reading

Before you can *write* academically, you need to know how to *read* academically.

The seven stage method below should assist you in this process. Take any journal article or chapter in a text book and read it through from beginning to end.

This example uses the open access article at:

http://www.hindawi.com/journals/edri/2015/209154/

(A different example appears on the companion website, which demonstrates the reading process step by step).

Education Research International
Volume 2015 (2015), Article ID 209154, 14 pages
http://dx.doi.org/10.1155/2015/209154

Research Article

A Study on the Relationship between English Reading Comprehension and English Vocabulary Knowledge

Yu-han Ma and Wen-ying Lin

Department of English Instruction, University of Taipei, Taipei 100, Taiwan

Received 15 July 2014; Revised 18 December 2014; Accepted 26 December 2014

Academic Editor: Yi-Shun Wang

Copyright © 2015 Yu-han Ma and Wen-ying Lin. This is an open access article distributed under the Creative Commons Attribution License, which permits unrestricted use, distribution, and reproduction in any medium, provided the original work is properly cited.

- 🗎 Abstract
- 🗎 Full-Text PDF
- 🗎 Full-Text HTML
- 🗎 Full-Text ePUB
- 🗎 Full-Text XML
- 🗎 Linked References
- ? How to Cite this Article

For each article you read, write down notes for each of the seven sections:

1. What is this article about?	Language understanding; international students' language development.
2. What is the author's focus?	That knowledge of vocabulary is a prerequisite for successful reading comprehension
3. What *evidence* does the author present to support this focus?	Huang's study; Wu and Hu's study; Taiwanese students' performance in TOEIC (Test of English for International Communication)
4. What is the opposing/ supporting evidence?	Meara – vocabulary requires breadth and depth; Qian – vocabulary has 4 dimensions (multidimensional); Schmitt – claims native English speakers use similar lexicons; Clark – instability of the testing; Read – developed an alternative word association test; Ellis – claimed that large chunks of text are memorised;
5. Do you agree or disagree with the views expressed by the author? Why? (See actual research and conclusions)	*(Write down your views here)*
6. Useful linking words	compared; consistently found; noted; concluded; suggested; contended; employed; proposed; focused; illustrated; examined; claimed; have shown; reported; pointed out; asserted;

7. Choose three references from this text and start the process again	Qian, D.D. (2002). Assessing the roles of depth and breadth of vocabulary knowledge and academic reading performance: an assessment perspective. *Language Learning, vol. 52, no. 3, pp. 523-536.*
	Read, J. (2002). Assessing Vocabulary, Cambridge University Press, Cambridge, UK.
	Schmitt, N. and Meara, P. (2011). Researching vocabulary through a word knowledge framework: word associations and verbal suffixes. Studies in Second Language Acquisition, vol.19, pp. 17-36.

*More examples on the companion website **www.studentspaceuk.com**

So far you have developed a few strategies and tools to assist in the learning process by performing effective web searches and thinking like your teacher. Now it's time to take stock and ensure that you develop the confidence to build on what you already know. Always remember, that when you were five years old, you didn't know that you didn't know how to drive a car! Sometimes it's the not knowing what you don't know that is the problem, so by learning different ways of developing strategies in small bite sized chunks, you will build confidence, skill and knowledge in any area of your choosing, and whilst not your original intention, at least you now know a bit about chromatography!

SECTION 4

HEALTH AND WELLBEING

SECTION 4 – Health and Wellbeing

This section will cover the following:

- To drink or not to drink alcohol – that is the question?
- Exam Stress
- Planning for Life/Work/ Learning
- Looking after the Voice
- Engaging with Physical Activity
- Sleep and Rest
- Home and Away Food
- Even More Free Stuff
- Consequences

The content of this section may seem strange in relation to being a successful learner, but looking after both your mind and body will ensure that you are (and you remain) in tip-top condition to engage with the learning process.

To drink or not to drink alcohol – that is the question?

If you live in a country that permits the purchase and consumption of alcohol and that you meet the legal age requirement to do so, then this section has some very important advice.

So you are a student, possibly living away from home with some money up front in the form of a student loan or sponsorship. You are excited by this new adventure and the temptation to go out socialising, spending money on cheap alcohol can be tempting! It is worthwhile taking a step back and considering the consequences of these actions, as too much alcohol can affect your overall health and wellbeing.

If you don't believe this, watch these two short videos at:

https://www.youtube.com/watch?v=l-SBR7p7K-M

and

https://www.youtube.com/watch?v=-oN2emCHMlg

Alcohol is an addictive substance and consumption of large quantities in a single day/evening can have the same catastrophic effect on your body and subsequent long term health as if you were consuming smaller quantities socially over a longer period of time. Consumption of alcohol affects us both mentally and physically. In moderation, the odd alcoholic drink may be processed by your body without long term effect; however, following some basic simple advice will ensure that your body can process what is required without undue risk to your health.

- Intersperse alcoholic drinks with drinking water (or non-alcoholic drink)

- Experiment with a range of non-alcoholic cocktails or long fruit juices. Some of these can be more expensive than alcoholic drinks (particularly non-alcoholic cocktails). Ordering these will not make you stand out in a crowd that is drinking alcohol; but if you think it does, then dare to be different.

Like most things we eat and drink, moderation and careful management of intake is preferable to allow your body to process what is consumed. When we abuse our body we put ourselves and others at risk. If you choose to drink alcohol, manage your alcohol consumption wisely.

Should you wish further information about alcohol consumption and related issues, visit:

http://www.drinkaware.co.uk

http://www.nhs.uk/Tools/Pages/Toolslibrary.aspx

Exam Stress

We all experience the normal anxieties associated with assessment and exams. Most of us work through these anxieties without difficulty, but for some, this can be an unsettling time.

Exam induced stress causes a negative impact on the health and wellbeing of students, so it is important to be aware of the symptoms and the simple strategies that may personally work in managing this effectively.

What are the symptoms of exam induced stress? The symptoms are no different from those related to stress and can be divided into four areas:

(i) Physical (ii) Emotional (iii) Cognitive and (iv) Behavioural.

(i) Physical stress is perhaps the most straightforward to identify as it relates to stress hormones being released into the body causing sweaty palms, increased heart rate, headaches or tight shoulders.

(ii) Emotional stress can cause the onset of negative feelings, hopelessness and depression.

(iii) Cognitive stress can cause the lack of concentration, becoming unfocused and unable to engage with problem-solving activities with clarity. Some may also experience sound or light sensory irritation.

(iv) Behavioural stress can cause changes to eating habits, affect normal sleep patterns and can also stop you talking to friends and becoming withdrawn.

Managing Exam Stress

Some simple and effective ways to manage exam related stress can be drawn from the information within the topics elsewhere within this section. An effective way to minimise impact on your body and mind is through healthy eating and exercise. Fast foods, snacking and irregular eating habits give your body an energy shock through carbohydrate or sugar overload but are not as effective as more nutritious (longer lasting) energy foods. If you have an established regular exercise routine throughout the year, it is important to keep this going prior to and during your exam schedule. If you have not engaged with regular exercise, then a brisk walk ending with some deep and slow breaths can prove to be effective. Check out some useful advice on exam stress from the resources section of the Student Minds website **http://www.studentminds.org.uk/exam-stress.html**

Planning for Life/Work/Learning

At school, college and university you will hear about aims, objectives, outcomes, short term planning, medium term planning, long term planning and personal planning. All are important and necessary, but the only person who can determine effective planning for life/work/learning is YOU. At its very essence, the following may be a good starting guide and as a rule of thumb works very well in relation to managing and engaging with any learning session.

Personal Planning – maintaining a cool head

In order to consider how your life/work/learning is going to be planned and managed, you need to consider fixed calendar events over which you have no control.

Your holidays! - get a year planner and write in all your holidays. Between each holiday, mark out the number of weeks/sessions/days that you have and what your overall aim is for that period of time. For example, you may have 6 weeks to complete a learning topic. Whatever your endpoint is, that is your overall AIM of what you hope to achieve.

Learning Context – (Consider this in the context of YOU planning a learning session or YOU attending a session planned by someone else).

- what is the subject/theme/concept/unit title of the learning with which you will engage?
- who will assist in this context? What are the names of the teachers (assistants/helpers)?
- duration of learning session?
- where does this learning session fit in the grand scheme of things (is it a one-off session or part of a series)?
- what do you know already and what might you need to find out before attending the session?
- where will the session take place (room number)?
- what materials might you be required to bring to the session?

Abraham Maslow identified a theory of human needs and motivation that is commonly used in relation to learning. The theory is straight forward to understand and begins to make sense in relation to our basic human need to learn. If you are interested in exploring this further you can access information from the companion website at **http://www.studentspaceuk.com**

Learning Content –

- What is in the syllabus and what is the big picture (the overall aim/goal) for the learning content?
- What is the subject content, (topics, themes)?
- What are the aims/objectives/learning intentions?

Learning product – How can your learning be demonstrated effectively? What are the activities and type of assessments with which you will engage?

Learning process –

- What will be the format (presentation; investigation; dialogue)?
- room arrangement (physical layout)
- learning arrangement (small groups; large group; individual)

Learning outline/plan – Consider how you should prepare for each learning session. Be aware that lessons are normally constructed in three parts (i) starter – this can be a link to previous learning sessions, but generally introduces and contextualises what is to be covered; (ii) main - this is the new knowledge that is being explored; (iii) Plenary – a summary of what has been covered and a check that new concepts and knowledge have been embedded. Sometimes there is time to ask questions too, so it is important that you are present for the whole learning session. If you miss anything though lateness or absence, then it is your responsibility to catch up on missed content. Teachers will be more accommodating if you attempt to demonstrate that you have an awareness of the content you have missed, should you seek out the possibility of a catch up session. Lastly, and more importantly, if you require any form of assistive technology or other learning assistance then you should ensure that this is known well in advance and that it is your responsibility to ensure that such assistance is available to you.

Reflection – It is always good practice to reflect on anything with which you engage; so reflect on:

- what new learning took place
- how did this enhance your current knowledge?
- Did this learning raise any questions?

It is a good idea to write this down somewhere, so that you can check over, contextualise and make sense of your new learning. If your reflection raises further questions, try to answer these yourself by using your investigative skills on the world wide web, or by seeking out other sources.

Looking after the Voice

The voice is the most overlooked muscle in our body and indeed the most abused, so it is important that we ensure that we look after this essential communication tool. Vocal health is not something exclusively within the domain of actors and singers, but within all of us.

Some simple things to consider:

- Avoid shouting. You may raise your voice occasionally, but it is more beneficial to adopt other strategies that will allow you to communicate in the normal pitch and volume of your voice

- Think about your breathing. It is important to develop control of your air intake as well as ensuring that you have a good posture. Try some breathing exercises along with some relaxation exercises. It may sound odd, but if you try out some simple vocal exercises as a warm up to your day, your voice will respond accordingly. Doing vocal exercises whilst you are in the shower is not a daft idea!

Try out the following breathing challenge as a daily morning routine when taking a shower. Steam and moisture from the shower is beneficial when inhaled through the mouth and nose: however, the challenge is to breathe in through your nose and exhale (audibly) through an open mouth whilst keeping a steady finger click. Count the finger clicks until you break the continuous exhale. Your challenge is to increase the number of clicks at the next shower. At the end of each shower breathing challenge you should relax by quietly humming. Have fun doing this and your vocal health will improve. Do not be surprised to find that the length of your controlled (audible) exhale will increase over time. This shower workout will also keep your lung capacity healthy.

- Keep your throat lubricated. Drink plenty throughout the day (avoid fizzy drinks or squashes as they can increase dehydration – plain water is best); throat lozenges also cause dehydration so they are not recommended, but sucking a soft fruit gum will help by coating the throat with glycerine and will slow down the dehydration process. Drinking a whipped egg white is ideal if you have to make a presentation (or sing). This is what the professionals do if their voice is a bit rough.

- Do not stretch the pitch or volume of the voice when 'cold'. That is when you first waken up in the morning or when moving to areas of distinctively different temperatures. Ensure your body temperature is even. There is some truth in the old wife's tale of wrapping up to avoid catching colds and sore throats. The truth relates to keeping an even body temperature. The vocal chords do not respond well to changes in temperature and the initial stages of body shock, which can contribute to the development of a rough throat and cough.

Think of the scenario of a queue of people waiting to get into a night club. The weather is dry but cold and most of those who are queuing are shivering. Shivering is an early stage of body shock and this along with a sudden move into a warmer temperature causes the vocal chords to spasm – well it is a muscle – and muscle spasms are not pleasant and put stress on the body. So the simple solution is to make sure your body is wrapped up and warm in cold temperatures and remove outside clothing when inside in a warmer temperature. Too many keep on an outside coat whilst inside a building so the body never acclimatises to the change in temperature.

Engaging with Physical Activity

Most of us, sadly, will have been more physically active when we were children through running and playing games. In the current world of electronic games there is a growing concern that as children become adolescents and subsequently adults, physical inactivity becomes the norm. Swimming, sport activities and gym workouts are all commendable, but there are some simple, obvious things that you can do on a daily basis that will contribute to your physical fitness. Try walking for fitness each day. If you use public transport, then walking will be part of that activity; however, look for ways of increasing your walk and if it involves an uphill incline - then all to the good. If your form of public transport is a bus, then get off a stop or two early and walk. Always take the stairs going up rather than using a lift. If you drive a car to a local shop – leave the car at base and walk there and back. Consider cycling as this is an excellent physical activity. Think of those who meet the challenge of not being able to use their limbs at all. They think it second nature to remain physically active and they work around their challenges on a daily basis. The mix of physical activity within our work/lifestyle balance is essential and you will find that you are more willing to engage with learning activities. Think smart!

If you would like to explore Pilates or Workout activities, check out the free videos on the companion website at **http://www.studentspaceuk.com**

Sleep and Rest

We are all aware (and have experience) of the effect of tiredness on our bodies and when you are tired, you are unable to concentrate sufficiently. Physical tiredness is where our muscles ache after physical activity (over exertion) and mental tiredness is where we are unable to accept any further sensory information (sight and hearing).

In most cases, both physical and mental tiredness are interlinked and can be felt at the same time. In the case of physical activity, planned bursts can have a positive impact on brain activity. Sport, swimming and gym activity can all impact positively on brain function, but the key to success is ensuring that these are planned for specific lengths of time to avoid over exertion. Engaging with some form of short burst physical activity is preferable to no engagement at all. This is explored later in this section.

Making sure that your body receives enough sleep and rest is vital for work/ life balance; however, it is not an exact science as we all require different lengths of sleep time and frequency of rest. Teenagers require 9¼ hours sleep to function best with some only requiring 8½ hours. Adults (ages between 18 and 25) function best with between 7 and 9 hours sleep with many requiring between 6 and 10 hours. How many hours of sleep are you currently managing to have? The guide for you will be what your body indicates. When you feel refreshed in the morning, how much sleep did you manage to have? Most of us will have what is known as deep sleep for between 3 to 4 hours. The remainder of the time will be rest sleep (both vital in the accumulated sleep hours). What also guarantees quality sleep, is how your room is laid out (tidy and free from clutter); level of ventilation; room temperature; comfort of the bed mattress; freshness of the bedding and pillows. Have you ever wondered why you seem to sleep better when you have clean bedding and pillows? Remember also to turn or flip the mattress as recommended by the manufacturer. It is not a daft idea to vacuum both sides of the mattress regularly. We shed a considerable amount of skin which serves as a gourmet meal for micro-world creatures that …. well we won't dwell on this …….!

You can boost your energy by taking a Power Nap. Many organisations require their workforce to engage with this and there is now wider debate on the benefits of a power nap in relation to quality learning for students.

Power naps last no longer than 20 minutes and ideally should be taken immediately after lunch. Once the timed 20 minutes is over, get back to action by confirming with your body that the nap is over. Splash some water in your face or jump up and down on the spot. Whatever you do, get right back into the task in hand whatever this might be. Have a look at the website **http:// www.sleep.org** by the Sleep Foundation to pick up some useful tips about snooze foods; beverages; pick me ups, winding down at the end of the day and learn more about sleep.

Home and Away Food

Sustenance for both body and mind is important and the balance of what is consumed should be nutritious. You do not need to be a master chef contestant or spend too much money to create nutritious meals. All that is required is a willingness to spend a little time purchasing the ingredients and preparing the meal. It is more fun if you can get like-minded people to share a meal with you – after all it should be a social occasion too. Here is a recipe for a very simple meal – The Student Chickpea Curry. (If you are not one for following recipes, check out the video on the companion website http:// studentspaceuk.com – there are more recipes for other meals too)

Student Chickpea Curry

Ingredients:

2 tins chickpeas (drained)

1 tin mushrooms (drained) or fresh mushrooms

½ bag of frozen onions (or one chopped fresh onion)

1 bag frozen spinach (or bag of fresh washed spinach)

¼ bag of frozen peppers (or use 1 fresh green pepper)

½ jar of curry paste (Korma or Bhuna) or quarter jar of both

1 tin chopped tomatoes

Some creamed coconut or coconut milk if you are feeling particularly decadent!

Method:

Fry the onions and peppers. Drain fluid from the mushrooms and the chickpeas (and rinse chickpeas under the cold tap). Add to the fried onions and peppers. Add tin tomatoes, curry paste and spinach (some creamed coconut or coconut milk if you wish). Ready in five minutes. Serve with rice or naan bread.

Even More Free Stuff

Yummly is a fantastic site for every recipe that appears on the web.	**http://www.yummly.com**
Better Movers, better thinkers resource pack.	**http://www.educationscotland.gov.uk/ Images/BMT_tcm4-868624.pdf**
LGBT – help and support.	**http://www.liveitwell.org.uk/support-help/lgbt/#National**
Sexual health.	**http://www.c4urself.org.uk/**
Open university – free study skills resources.	**http://www.open.edu/openlearn/ education**
Free toolkits for planning.	**http://www.jobs.ac.uk/careers-advice/ resources/ebooks-and-toolkits**
Free teaching and learning resources.	**http://www.learnhigher.ac.uk/**
Internet sources for teachers.	**http://www.strath.ac.uk/library/ yoursubjectlibrarian/hasslibrarians/ schools/**
Find anything… about…. for….	**http://bigpictureeducation.com/ resources**

Consequences

In Chinese philosophy of Yin and Yang, opposites are described as independent, complementary and interconnected. Within the laws of physics (motion), Sir Isaac Newton claimed *"For every action there is an equal and opposite reaction"*. The law of Karma (cause and effect) opens up Newton's law to all aspects of life, beyond just physical motion.

Whether personal belief systems link with Yin and Yang and/or Karma or both, it cannot be ignored that everything we think, speak and choose to action has subsequent consequences.

We do not always think about consequences until it is too late and then ponder…"I should not have said that …" or "wish I had done that differently! " Equally, we cannot go through life worrying about the 'what if'. We all need to engage in a certain amount of risk taking – otherwise our lives would become boring.

A balance is required by thinking through possible consequences whilst rehearsing the level of risk that might be involved. Once this has been done, an informed decision may be reached. An informed decision is based on further fact finding and forms the underpinning for your final decision.

Remember, informed decisions are always the right decisions made at that specific time. You may not make the same decision some years down the line, but personal life experiences help to shape views and opinions that contribute to our wider understanding of the world around us. This is called wisdom.

USEFUL LINKS
AND RESOURCES

USEFUL LINKS AND RESOURCES

All links from book sections can be found on the companion website **www.studentspaceuk.com** and on the StudentSpaceUK delicious account **http://delicious.com/StudentSpaceUk**

REFLECTION

REFLECTION

If you have landed on this page after engaging with the previous sections – well done! We hope that you found something useful to support and enhance your learning.

This book was not a quick fix or shortcut to becoming a successful learner. It was designed to empower you to engage more meaningfully with your personal learning. Your motivation to learn new things and increase your knowledge and skill will serve you well in all you may wish to achieve.

What is important, is acknowledging that learning requires a partnership between YOU and those responsible for leading learning. A successful outcome relies on what each brings to the learning sessions.

We hope that you will continue to develop your partnership with us, through registering with the companion website **www.studentspaceuk.com** Please send feedback or suggestions that could be incorporated in future editions of the book.

We hope you will share with us what you find useful.

So, for the present, we wish you every success.

Helen and Hugh